1　Greetings

Objectives

- To be able to exchange greetings properly.
- To be able to introduce yourself depending on the situation.

Greetings

	Formal	Informal
Morning	おはようございます。 Ohayô gozaimasu. (*Good morning.*)	おはよう。 Ohayô.
Afternoon	こんにちは。 Konnichiwa. (*Good afternoon.*)	
Evening	こんばんは。 Konbanwa. (*Good evening.*)	
Others	さようなら。／しつれいします。 Sayônara. / Shitsurê shimasu. (*See you.*)	じゃあ、また。／じゃあね。／バイバイ。／おさきに。 Jâ, mata. / Jâne. / Baibai. / Osakini. (*See you. / Bye.*)
	ありがとうございます。／すみません。 Arigatô gozaimasu. / Sumimasen. (*Thank you.*)	ありがとう。／どうも。 Arigatô. / Dômo. (*Thanks.*)
	すみません。／ごめんなさい。 Sumimasen. / Gomennasai. (*I am sorry.*)	ごめん。 Gomen. (*Sorry.*)
	すみません。 Sumimasen. (*Excuse me.*)	

Morning

Student：おはようございます。
　　　　　Ohayô gozaimasu.
　　　　　(*Good morning.*)

Teacher：おはようございます。
　　　　　Ohayô gozaimasu.
　　　　　(*Good morning.*)

Going back to home

Student：さようなら。／ しつれいします。
　　　　　Sayônara. / Shitsurê shimasu.
　　　　　(*See you.*)

Teacher：さようなら。
　　　　　Sayônara.
　　　　　(*See you.*)

Introduce yourself

Simple version

はじめまして。
Hajimemashite.
(*How do you do?*)

［*Name*］　です。
［*Name*］　desu.
(*I'm [Name].*)

どうぞ　よろしく。
Dôzo yoroshiku.
(*Nice to meet you.*)

Longer version

はじめまして。
Hajimemashite.
(*How do you do?*)

［*Name*］　です。
［*Name*］　desu.
(*I'm [Name].*)

せんもん　は　［*Your major*］　です。
Senmon　wa　［*Your major*］　desu.
(*My major is [Your major].*)

［*Favorite things*］　が　すき　です。
［*Favorite things*］　ga　suki　desu.
(*I like [Favorite things].*)

どうぞ　よろしく。
Dôzo yoroshiku.
(*Nice to meet you.*)

Conversation

A : おなまえ　は？

Onamae wa?

(*May I ask your name, please?*)

B : ［*Name*］　です。

［*Name*］　desu.

(*I'm [Name].*)

A : おくに　は？

Okuni wa?

(*What country are you from?*)

B : ［*Country name*］　から　きました。

［*Country name*］　kara　kimashita.

(*I came from [Country name].*)

A : あ　そうですか。

A sôdesuka.

(*Oh, I see.*)

せんもん　は？

Senmon wa?

(*What is your major?*)

B : ［*Your major*］　です。

［*Your major*］　desu.

(*My major is [Your major].*)

A : そうですか。

Sôdesuka.

(*I see.*)

1 Documents

Keywords

お名前（Onamae），氏名（Shimei）	Name
ふりがな（Furigana），フリガナ（Furigana）	Phonetic Japanese
おところ（Otokoro），住所（Jûsho）	Address
郵便番号（Yûbin bangô），〒□□□-□□□□	Postal code
電話番号（Denwa bangô），TEL	Phone number
性別（Sêbetsu），男（Otoko）／女（Onna）	Sex, Male/ Female
生年月日（Sênengappi）	Date of Birth
在留資格（Zairyûshikaku）	Status of residence
在留カード（Zairyûkâdo）	Residence card
国籍・地域（Kokuseki・Chiiki）	Nationality・Region
本人（Honnin）	Principal
続柄（Tsuzukigara）	Relationship to the householder

Western calendar and Japanese calendar

Year　Month　Day

The Japanese calendar is based on the number of years the emperor has been in rule.
Ex. 昭和（Showa），平成（Heisei）

1980年	昭和55年	1996年	平成8年	2012年	平成24年
1981年	昭和56年	1997年	平成9年	2013年	平成25年
1982年	昭和57年	1998年	平成10年	2014年	平成26年
1983年	昭和58年	1999年	平成11年	2015年	平成27年
1984年	昭和59年	2000年	平成12年	2016年	平成28年
1985年	昭和60年	2001年	平成13年	2017年	平成29年
1986年	昭和61年	2002年	平成14年	2018年	平成30年
1987年	昭和62年	2003年	平成15年	2019年	平成31年
1988年	昭和63年	2004年	平成16年	2020年	
1989年	昭和64年/平成元年	2005年	平成17年	2021年	
1990年	平成2年	2006年	平成18年	2022年	
1991年	平成3年	2007年	平成19年	2023年	
1992年	平成4年	2008年	平成20年	2024年	
1993年	平成5年	2009年	平成21年	2025年	
1994年	平成6年	2010年	平成22年	2026年	
1995年	平成7年	2011年	平成23年	2027年	

Ward office documents

平成　　　年度

記号番号　青葉　　　－

国民健康保険料軽減適用申告書
Declaration for reduction of National Health Insurance Premiums

年 Year	月 Month	日 Day

仙台市青葉区長
To the Director of the Aoba Ward Office

私の世帯の収入について次のとおり申告します。
I declare my households' total income as follows.

※ローマ字で記入していただいて構いません。
You may fill it in using romaji (English alphabet).

世 帯 主 氏 名 Name of head of household	姓 Surname　　　　名 Given name　　　Middle name	電話番号 Phone Number
住　　　　　所 Address in Japan		

同一世帯を構成する者 Household Members

氏　　　　　名 Names			
生 年 月 日 Date of birth	年 Year　　月 Month　日 Day	年 Year　　月 Month　日 Day	年 Year　　月 Month　日 Day
入 国 目 的 Purpose of entry	☐ 留学生 Student　　☐ その他 Other	☐ 留学生 Student　　☐ その他 Other	☐ 留学生 Student　　☐ その他 Other
昨年中の日本での収入 Income earned in Japan last year	なし（新規入国のため） None(new resident to Japan)		

※国民健康保険料は、加入している世帯員数と前年中の収入、加入期間に応じて計算されます。
Your insurance premium is calculated based on the number of household members, total household income of the previous year, and length of enrollment in the national health insurance scheme.

※初年度の保険料は、昨年日本での収入がなかった場合70％軽減されます。
Your first year's insurance premium can be reduced by 70 % if you did not have any income in the previous year.

※今後収入が発生したり世帯員数が増加した場合、翌年度以降の保険料が大きく変わることがあります。
Your insurance premium after next year is subject to change if you earn an income or the number of household members increases.

処理欄	戸籍住民課	受付年月日　平成　年　月　日		
	保険年金課	入力年月日　平成　年　月　日	入力結果　☐ 非課税　☐ 非課税引継	入 力 担 当 者　軽 減 判 定　　　割

外国人住民用	住民票の写しなどの交付請求書	戸・印・登

時　分

（あて先）仙台市　　　区長

同日住所異動届

注意

●プライバシーの侵害につながるような不当な目的による請求には応じられません。
●偽り、その他不正な手段により交付を受けたときは、三十万円以下の罰金に処せられます。
●代理人又は使者、若しくはその他の方が請求する場合は、請求者本人自署の委任状が必要です。
●消えにくい筆記用具により、太枠の中だけ記入してください。

① どなたの証明が必要ですか

交付請求年月日　平成　　年　　月　　日

住　所 Address	仙台市		□連記
	方書・建物名		
氏　名 Name		Date of birth　　年　　月　　日生 Year　Month　Day	□各々

※ 世帯の一部でご請求の際は必要な方の氏名をご記入願います

② 何通必要ですか

住民票の写し	世 帯 全 員	通	除　　　票	通
	本 人 の み	通	記載事項証明書	通
	世 帯 の 一 部	通		

③ 記載項目のご指定と請求事由　　☑印を付けてください

【！】指定されない項目は記載が省略されます

右枠内の項目
□ すべて記載
□ 記載項目を指定
　（右枠内で指定してください）

⇒

□ 国籍・地域
□ 在留の区分
　（法30条の45に規定する区分）
□ 在留カード等の番号

□ 在留資格※1.
　在留期間等※1.
　在留期間満了の日※1.
　※1.個別の指定はできません

□ 続柄
□ 通称の履歴
□ 氏名のカタカナ表記
□ 以前の住所　※2.

□ 住民票コード※3.　□ 個人番号※3.
※3. 本人・同一世帯員のみ請求可
※3. 住民票コード・個人番号が記載された証明書の提出には法的制限がありますので，ご注意願います。

※2.必要とする住所をご記入ください

請求事由（何の手続きで，どちらに提出されるかをご記入ください）

	5
外固有・続柄	4
続柄のみ	3
外固有のみ	2
すべて省略	1
履歴	
住民票コード 記載	2
住民票コード 省略	1
マイNo. 記載	2
マイNo. 省略	1
外国人固有項目	
すべて記載	
個別指定	
国籍・地域	2
在留区分	2
在留情報	2
在力等番号	2
通称履歴	2
氏名カタカナ表記	2

④ 窓口にお越しの方（請求者）　　☑印を付けて必要事項をご記入ください

□ 本　人 ※除票の請求時のみ現住所をご記入ください	現住所	
□ 同一世帯員	住所	
□ 代 理 人		
□ そ の 他 ※法人請求者は代表者印を押印願います	フリガナ 氏　名	①との関係
□ 使　者 ※法人請求で、窓口に起こしの方が請求者本人ではない場合には、お越しの方について記入願います	住所	
	フリガナ 氏　名	請求者との関係

本人確認	口頭質問（確認・未確認）　※裏面有	金　額	受付	作成	認証
番カ・住B・免・パ・在・特・学・障・他（写真有：　　　） ■・国・社・共・年・介・前・後・他（写真なし：　　　）		00 円			

再生紙使用

1

総合口座利用申込書（Suica用）

通常貯金預入申込書（新規）
振替口座加入申込書・オートスウィング利用申込書

ご新規

※ご記入の前に本申込書裏面をお読みください。
※太枠からはみ出さないようにボールペンではっきりとご記入ください。☑枠欄は、該当の項目にレ印をつけてください。
※「おなまえ」の姓と名の間（法人の方は会社の種類と会社名の間）は、1文字分空けてご記入ください。なお、「フリガナ」の会社の種類と会社名の間はつめてご記入ください。
※濁点、半濁点は別のマスを使用せず1マスにご記入ください。

おところ

郵便番号 ☐☐☐ － ☐☐☐☐

電話番号 ☐☐☐☐☐ － ☐☐☐☐ － ☐☐☐☐ ⚠ 左詰めでご記入ください。

おなまえ

フリガナ

様

生年月日 または 設立年月日	☐ 明治　☐ 大正　☐ 昭和　☐ 平成　☐☐ 年　☐☐ 月　☐☐ 日	金額	千万 百万 十万 万 千 百 十 円

⚠ 金額の頭部に「￥」をご記入ください。

Suica付カード申込みのお客さま

カードの種類	性別（Suica付カードのみ）→	同意事項		Suica同意欄
☐ JP BANKカード		ゆうちょICキャッシュカードSuicaをお申込みのお客さまは、この申込書の裏面の記載事項をご確認いただき、同意の上、押印してください。（押印がない場合は、ゆうちょICキャッシュカードSuicaのお申込みはできません。）		印
☐ Suica付カード	☐ 男　☐ 女	私は「ゆうちょICキャッシュカードSuica規定」、「ゆうちょICキャッシュカードSuica利用特約」及び本申込書裏面の「個人情報のお取扱い」を同意の上、ゆうちょICキャッシュカードSuicaを申し込みます。		
☐ 一般カード				
☐ 利用しない	⚠「JP BANKカード」をご希望の場合、この申込書のほか、「キャッシュカード機能あり JP BANKカード」専用の申込書の提出が必要です。窓口へお申し出ください。（簡易郵便局または、郵送でのお申込みの場合は選択できません）			

口座種類	☐ 通常　☐ 貯蓄	ボランティア	☐ 国際協力（全般）　☐ 国際協力（環境）　☐ 申し込まない	オートスウィング基準額	千万 百万 十万 万 千 百 十 円

⚠ 金額の頭部に「￥」をご記入ください。

キャッシュサービス利用方法	☐ 通帳とカード　☐ カードのみ	デビット機能	☐ 利用する　☐ 利用しない

暗証番号必須取扱い	☐ 申し込む　☐ 申し込まない	法人番号	☐☐☐☐☐☐☐☐☐☐☐☐☐

＜取扱店使用欄＞

備考		取引区分	個　人 :1　OCR必須	取引時確認区分	本・代・法・人・顧
			課 税 法 人（預入制限 有）:3		本人確認資料 免許証等:1（郵送確認不要）住民票等:2（郵送確認要）
			非課税法人（預入制限 有）:4		
			課 税 法 人（預入制限なし）:5		
			非課税法人（預入制限なし）:6		

モード	暗証なし:1 暗証設定:2	OCR必須 送金機能 なし:2	用紙番号 ☐☐☐☐	OCR必須 ☐☐☐☐☐☐	翌日本締	報告番号 合同預入 ☐☐☐☐	預入限度額 ☐ オートスウィング基準額 ☐ キャッシュカード説明 ☐	検査	取引時確認	受付

（1枚目）**OCR用**　　（取扱郵便局・取扱店→受持貯金事務センター）　　チ 60210（27-TPN）　**JP ゆうちょ銀行**

非居住者等届書

年　月　日

独立行政法人郵便貯金・簡易生命保険管理機構が管理する郵便貯金については、同機構に届出します。
※太枠内にボールペンではっきりとご記入ください。

おなまえ又は名称	フリガナ
	様

届出をする貯金の記号番号	記　号	⚠	番　号

⚠通帳に記載のある方のみご記入ください。

利子の還付先の通常貯金記号番号	記　号	⚠	番　号

⚠通帳に記載のある方のみご記入ください。

※□枠欄は、該当の項目にレ印をつけてください。

届出区分	□居住者への変更
	□非居住者への変更（非居住者）
	□非居住者への変更（外国法人）

個人の場合	国外のおところ又は居所	
	日中ご連絡先電話番号	携帯　会社　自宅
	国　籍	
	入国年月日	年　月　日

法人の場合	本店又は主たる事務所の所在地	
	日中ご連絡先電話番号	ー　　ー
	設立又は組織された場所	
	事業が管理・支配されている場所	
	日中ご連絡先電話番号	ー　　ー　担当者
	設立年月日	年　月　日

居住者として課税される国及び納税地	（納税者番号　　　　　）

日本国内の恒常的施設所持の状況	□あり	名　称	
		所在地	
	□なし		

外交特権所持の状況	□あり　　□なし

＜お客さまへの確認事項＞
　本日から1週間以内に他行あてに振り込みの予定がある場合は、□枠欄にレ印をつけてください。　□

日附印

＜取扱店使用欄＞

税率	所得税		電話連絡	振込予定がある場合のJCへの連絡日時等	連絡者	備考	受付
	地方税						

（取扱郵便局・取扱店→原簿管理貯金事務センター）【規程Naviコード：50306　改正年月：2016.1】　ゆうちょ銀行

2 Campus Tour Challenge

Objectives

- To learn the locations of university facilities.
- To understand Kawauchi campus better.

Welcome to Tohoku University's Kawauchi campus. You might have already heard or learned about the history, programs, etc. of our school. Now we would like to ask you to try this Campus Tour Challenge to prove you really know about this school. Through this campus tour, we hope you have fun, become familiar with our campus, and more importantly, fall in love with this university.

To pass this challenge, finish the following tasks:

1. Find the statue of this person, put a star on its location on the campus map and write down something about him (at least his major).

   My name is…..

   Courtesy of Tohoku University Archives

2. There are many club activities at Tohoku University. Find a gym on Kawauchi campus and tell us what people are doing there right now.

   People are….

3. Tohoku University has a Center for Learning Support (SLA). Find the center and get a brochure from there.

9

4. Find the Student Health Care Center and take a group photo in front of the center.

5. Go to Tohoku University Library and get a brochure from the reference desk.

6. Go to a cafeteria on Kawauchi campus and list 5 foods on the menu.

7. Go to the multimedia building and log in to a computer. Ask the Japanese students in your group about a famous sightseeing spot in Miyagi. Search for it online and print out a webpage about the sightseeing spot.

8. Ask the Japanese students in your group about their favorite spots on Kawauchi campus. Take photos of those spots.

東北大学 川内キャンパス
TOHOKU UNIVERSITY Kawauchi Campus

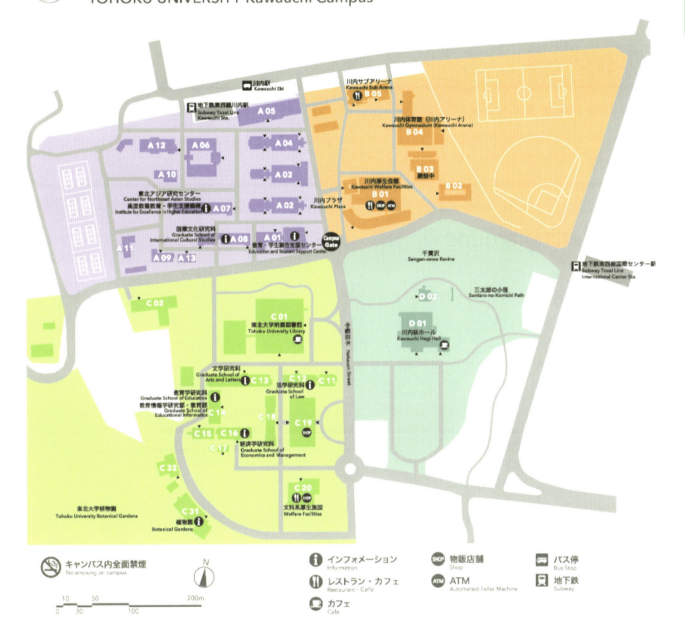

3 Shopping
At Convenience Stores, Supermarkets etc.

Objectives

- To be able to ask where things/places are.
- To be able to thank people.
- To be able to order food and drinks.

Getting around

Asking questions

[*Places* / *Things*] は　どこですか？　*Where is / are [places / things]?*
　　　　　　　　　　[*Places* / *Things*] wa　doko desuka?

スーパー　Sûpâ
(*Supermarket*)
コンビニ　Konbini
(*Convenience store*)
パン　Pan
(*Bread*)
ミルク　Miruku
(*Milk*)

Make a list of places / things you want to find:

-
-
-
-
-

Saying thank you
どうも。　Dômo.
ありがとうございます。　Arigatô gozaimasu.
すみません。Sumimasen.

12

In town①

Convenience store

Customer:	すみません。 Sumimasen.	*Excuse me.*
Clerk :	はい。 Hai.	*Yes?*
Customer:	[Things] は どこですか。 [Things] wa doko desuka.	*Where is/are [Things]?*
Clerk :	こちらです。どうぞ。 Kochira desu. Dôzo.	*This way please.*
Customer:	－どうも。Dômo. －ありがとうございます。Arigatô gozaimasu. －すみません。Sumimasen.	*Thanks.* *Thank you very much.* *Thank you.*
Clerk :	いいえ。 Iie.	*Not at all.*

Paying

Clerk :	[Price] えん で ございます。 [Price] en de gozaimasu.	*That's [Price] yen please..*
Customer:	<Pay in cash or by credit card>	
Clerk :	あたためますか。 Atatamemasu ka.	*Would you like it heated up?*
Customer:	－はい、おねがいします。 Hai, onegaishimasu. －いいえ。 Iie.	*Yes, please.* *No thank you.*
Clerk :	ありがとうございました。 Arigatô gozaimashita.	*Thank you very much.*

***

レジぶくろ　Reji bukuro (*Shopping bag*)
わりばし　Waribashi (*Disposable chopsticks*)
ストロー　Sutorô (*Straw*)
スプーン　Supûn (*Spoon*)
フォーク　Fôku (*Fork*)

おねがいします。
Onegaishimasu.
(*Please*)

Numbers

1	2	3	4	5
いち	に	さん	し/よん	ご
Ichi	Ni	San	Shi/Yon	Go

6	7	8	9	10
ろく	しち/なな	はち	きゅう/く	じゅう
Roku	Shichi/Nana	Hachi	Kyû/Ku	Jû

		1	*One*
		10	*Ten*
		100	*Hundred*
	1	000	*One thousand*
	10	000	*Ten thousand*
	100	000	*Hundred thousand*
1	000	000	*One million*
10	000	000	*Ten million*
100	000	000	*Hundred million*

		1	いち	Ichi
		10	じゅう	Jû
		100	ひゃく	Hyaku
		1000	せん	Sen
	1	0000	いちまん	Ichi man
	10	0000	じゅうまん	Jû man
	100	0000	ひゃくまん	Hyaku man
	1000	0000	せんまん	Sen man
1	0000	0000	いちおく	Ichi oku

¥10,000　=　1 万 円（いちまんえん）

Say 'ichi man' *for 10,000*

Vocabulary

ぶたにく 豚肉	Buta niku	*Pork*	さかな 魚	Sakana	*Fish*
とりにく 鶏肉	Tori niku	*Chicken*	やさい 野菜	Yasai	*Vegetable*
ぎゅうにく 牛肉	Gyû niku	*Beef*	たまご/たまご 卵／玉子	Tamago	*Egg*
さけ 酒	Sake	*Alcohol*	くだもの 果物	Kudamono	*Fruit*

In town ②

3

Ordering food and drinks

Customer:	すみません。[Items] おねがいします。	*Excuse me, [Items] please.*
	Sumimasen [Items] Onegaisimasu.	
Server :	はい。	*Certainly.*
	Hai	

＊＊＊＊＊＊＊＊＊＊

Server :	ごちゅうもんは おきまりですか？	*Are you ready to order?*
	Gochûmon wa okimari desuka?	
Customer:	一[Items] を [Number] つ おねがいします。	*May I have [Number] [Items]*
	[Items] o [Number] tsu onegaishimasu.	*please?*
	一[Items] を [Number] つと [Items] を [Number] つ おねがいします。	
	[Items] o [Number] tsu to [Items] o [Number] tsu onegaishimasu.	
Server :	かしこまりました。	*Certainly.*
	Kashikomarimashita	

＊＊

メニューMenyû (*Menu*)
みず Mizu (*Water*)   おねがいします。
おちゃ Ocha (*Tea*)

General counters

一つ	1つ	ひとつ	Hitotsu	*One item*
二つ	2つ	ふたつ	Futatsu	*Two items*
三つ	3つ	みっつ	Mittsu	*Three items*
四つ	4つ	よっつ	Yottsu	*Four items*
五つ	5つ	いつつ	Itsutsu	*Five items*
六つ	6つ	むっつ	Muttsu	*Six items*
七つ	7つ	ななつ	Nanatsu	*Seven items*
八つ	8つ	やっつ	Yattsu	*Eight items*
九つ	9つ	ここのつ	Kokonotsu	*Nine items*
十	1 0	とお	Tô	*Ten items*

ハンバーガーを 1つ おねがいします。
Hanbâgâ o hitotsu onegaishimasu.
A hamburger, please.

ハンバーガーを 1つ と サラダを 1つ おねがいします。
Hanbâgâ o hitotsu to sarada o hitotsu onegaishimasu.
A hamburger and a salad, please.

On campus

Cafeterias on Kawauchi campus

Kawauchi no Mori Dining
Hours: Weekday 08:00~20:00 / Saturday Sunday, and Holiday 11:00~14:30

Kitchen Terrace Couleur
Hours: Weekdays 08:00~15:00
*Halal food is available

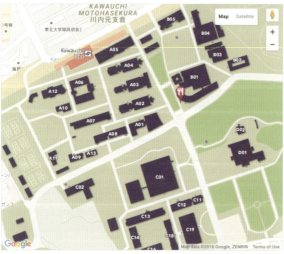

Bush Clover Café
Hours: Weekdays 7:50~17:00

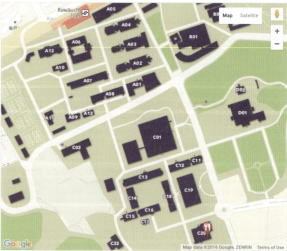

Kawauchi Co-op Restaurant
Hours: Weekdays 10:00~19:30, Sat. 11:00~13:30

Practice

Go to the cafeteria and order items from the menu.

4 Emergencies
Injury, Sickness

Objectives

- To be able to ask for help in Japanese when an emergency occurs.
- To be able to express where you are hurt in Japanese.

Tohoku University Emergency Contact Card

Emergency Contact Card	Emergency Contact Card
Name 氏名	Police 警察　110　　　Ambulance/Fire 救急車 / 消防署
Nationality 国籍　　　Date of Birth 生年月日	私は東北大学の留学生です。 東北大学附属病院に搬送してください。
Address 住所	I am an international student at Tohoku University. Please take me to Tohoku University Hospital.
Department 所属部局　　Supervisor 指導教員名	
Affiliation Contact (Email or Tel) 所属研究室連絡先	
Emergency Contact in Japan (Name & Tel) 緊急連絡先（日本国内）	
Tohoku University 東北大学	Tohoku University 東北大学

Do you have this card with you?

List of Embassy/Consulate/Representative Office

Bangladesh	(03)5704－0216	4-15-15 Meguro, Meguro-ku, Tokyo 東京都目黒区目黒 4-15-15
China	(025)228－8888	5220-18 Nishiôhatachô, Chûô-ku, Nîgata 新潟市中央区西大畑町 5220-18
France	(03)5798－6000	4-11-44 Nishiazabu, Minato-ku, Tokyo 東京都港区西麻布 4-11-44
Germany	(03)5791－7700	4-5-10 Minamiazabu, Tokyo 東京都南麻布 4-5-10
Indonesia	(03)3441－4201	5-2-9 Higashigotanda, Shinagawa-ku, Tokyo 東京都品川区東五反田 5-2-9
South Korea	(022)221－2751	1-4-3 Kamisugi, Aoba-ku, Sendai 仙台市青葉区上杉 1-4-3
Malaysia	(03)3476－3840	20-16 Nanpeidaichô, Shibuya-ku, Tokyo 東京都渋谷区南平台町 20-16
Taiwan	(03)3280－7800	5-20-2 Shirokanedai, Minato-ku, Tokyo 東京都港区白金台 5-20-2
Thailand	(03)5789－2433	3-14-6 Kamiôsaki, Shinagawa-ku, Tokyo 東京都品川区上大崎 3-14-6
U.S.A.	(011)641-1115	Kita 1-jô Nishi 28-chôme, Chûô-ku, Sapporo 札幌市中央区北一条西 28 丁目
Vietnam	(03)3466－3311	50-11 Motoyoyogichô, Shibuya, Tokyo 東京郡渋谷区元代々木町 50-11

On campus

Student Health Care Center
@Kawauchi North campus
(022) 795-7829

Internal medicine, Surgery, Mental health, Dentistry

Health Care Room
@Aobayama campus
(022) 795-3667

Internal medicine

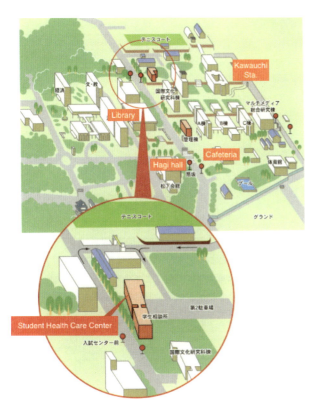

C05 工学部管理棟
Kôgakubu Kanritô
School of Engineering Administration Office
5th floor, Rm.510

すみません、保健管理センターはどこですか？

Sumimasen, hoken kanri sentâ wa doko desu ka?
(Excuse me, where is the Student Health Care Center?)

一緒に行ってください。

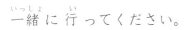

Issho ni itte kudasai.
(Could you please go with me?)

In town

Get attention

すみません！	Sumimasen!	*Excuse me!*
たすけて！	Tasukete!	*Help me!*
たいへん！	Taihen!	*Oh no!*

Ask someone to call

すみません、ここに電話してください。

Sumimasen, koko ni denwa site kudasai.

(Excuse me, please call this number.)

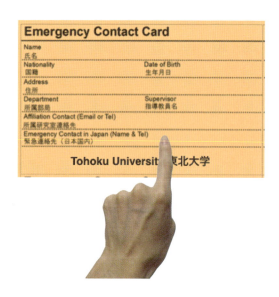
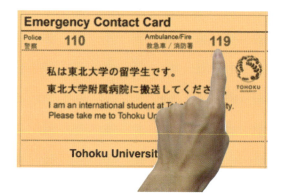

Explain the situation

交通事故です。

Kôtsûjiko desu.

(There's been a traffic accident.)

_____Body part_____が痛いです。

_____ga itai desu.

(My_____ hurts.)

ここが痛いです。

Koko ga itai desu.

(It hurts here.)

4

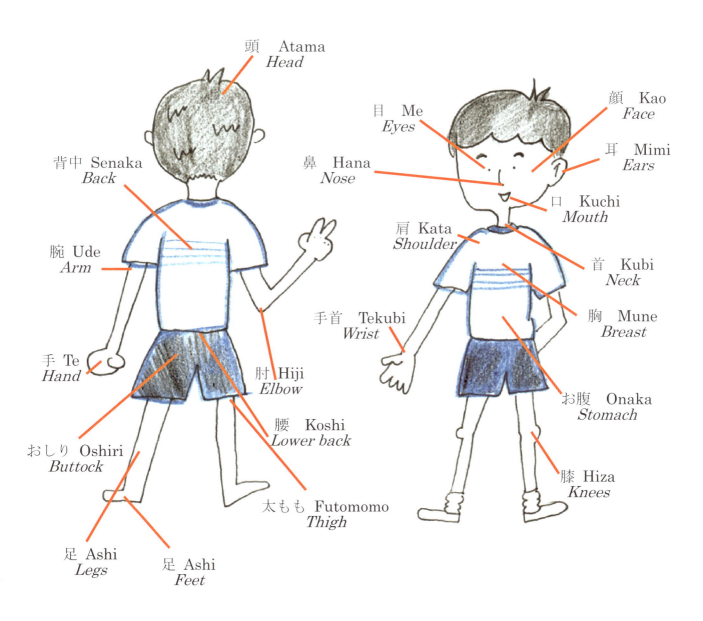

21

Practice

You and your friends go to a restaurant. A person at the table next to yours gets very drunk, suddenly begins vomiting, then falls over. No one at the same table notices. What should you do?

You are on your way home. Suddenly a bicycle hits you from behind. You fall over and cannot stand up because your whole body hurts. What should you do?

You are working at a café as a part-time job. While preparing food, you cut your finger and cannot stop the bleeding. No one is around right now as everyone is very busy serving food or taking orders. What should you do?

You and your friend go shopping in town. Suddenly your friend falls over and starts shaking. What should you do?

5 Natural Disasters
Earthquake, tsunami, storm, flood, typhoon, volcanic eruption

Objectives

- To understand what disasters might happen in Japan.
- To be able to evacuate when an earthquake occurs.
- To be able to use essential vocabulary.

What to do when an earthquake occurs

At home
Protect your head
Don't panic and don't rush outside
Extinguish any fires after tremors have weakened
Secure an exit by opening a door

Outside
Stay away from concrete block walls and vending machines
Watch out for falling objects such as signs and window glass

At school or in a shop
Protect your head
Watch out for falling objects
Don't panic and don't rush outside

In an elevator
Push the buttons for all floors and get off as soon as possible

What to do after tremors have settled down
Look around
Gather information from TV and radio
Watch out for tsunamis
Go to a safe, wide-open area
Call out to the people around you and help each other
If your home is not safe, go to a refuge area

<Reference>
Advice for Protecting Yourself in an Earthquake   URL: http://int.sentia-sendai.jp/saigai/download/bousai_e.pdf

Natural disasters in Japan

地震　Jishin　(*Earthquake*)

*A magnitude 9.0 struck on 11th March 2011 (Great East Japan Earthquake).

津波　Tsunami　(*Tsunami*)

*A 10 m wave struck Sendai after the Great East Japan Earthquake.
Courtesy of Kuji

大雨　Ôame　(*Storm*)

洪水　Kôzui　(*Flood*)

* Sendai Sta. was flooded by heavy rain on 8th September 2016.

台風　Taifû　(*Typhoon*)

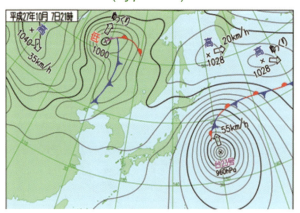

* There are many typhoons from August to October in Japan.
Courtesy of Japanese Meteorological Agency website
< http://www.jma.go.jp/jma/kishou/know/kurashi/tenkizu.html >

噴火　Funka　(*Volcanic eruption*)

* Near-crater warning was issued for Mt. Zao in 2015.

Emergency information

避難指示（緊急） Hinan shiji (Kinkyû) *Evacuation Order (Urgent)*	This notice is issued to order residents to evacuate as the risk of harm is imminent and the risk to residents' lives has increased.
避難勧告 Hinan kankoku *Evacuation Advisory*	This notice is issued to advise residents to evacuate due to the possibility of the area being affected by the disaster.
避難準備・高齢者等避難開始 Hinanjunbi・Kôreishatô hinankaishi *Notice to Prepare for Evacuation / Commence Evacuation for Elderly People*	This notice is issued to enable residents to prepare in advance to evacuate. Elderly and disabled people should use this as a guideline to commence voluntary evacuation.

<Reference> http://www.nic-nagoya.or.jp/en/nagoya_calendar/NIC_E_08-09_1710.pdf

Where is the closest evacuation area?

(Clue: schools)

仙台市災害多言語支援センター
Sendai Disaster Multilingual Support Center
@Sendai international center
Tel: (022) 224-1919, (022) 265-2471

25

Essential vocabulary

地震(じしん)	Jishin	*Earthquake*
津波(つなみ)	Tsunami	*Tsunami*
緊急(きんきゅう)	Kinkyû	*Emergency*
緊急地震速報(きんきゅうじしんそくほう)	Kinkyû jishin sokuhô	*Earthquake Early Warning*

Useful expressions

危(あぶ)ない！	Abunai!	*Watch out!*
はやく！	Hayaku!	*Hurry up!*
ダメ！	Dame!	*Stop!/Don't go there!*
逃(に)げろ！／逃(に)げて！	Nigero!/Nigete!	*Run away!*
走(はし)れ！／走(はし)って！	Hashire!/Hashitte!	*Run!*
待(ま)って！	Matte!	*Wait!/Hold on!*
行(い)かないで！	Ikanaide!	*Don't go!*
動(うご)かないで！	Ugokanaide!	*Don't move!*
入(はい)って！	Haitte!	*Come in!*
こっち・そっち・あっち	Kocchi・Socchi・Acchi	*Here/ There/ Over there*

* ～て ください　~te kudasai　*Please do~*
* ～ないで ください　~naide kudasai　*Please don't do~*

Vocabulary to know

震度 しんど	Shindo	*Scale of earthquake*
震源 しんげん	Shingen	*Earthquake epicenter*
余震 よしん	Yoshin	*Aftershock*
洪水 こうずい	Kôzui	*Flooding*
浸水 しんすい	Shinsui	*Water immersion*
ゲリラ 豪雨 ごうう	Gerira gôu	*Storm*
暴風雨 ぼうふうう	Bôfûu	*Rain storm*
崖崩れ がけくずれ	Gakekuzure	*Mudslide*
台風 たいふう	Taifû	*Typhoon*
噴火 ふんか	Funka	*Volcanic eruption*
避難 ひなん	Hinan	*Evacuation*
注意報 ちゅういほう	Chûihô	*Advisory, warning*
警報 けいほう	Kêhô	*Urgent warning*

Earthquake Early Warning System

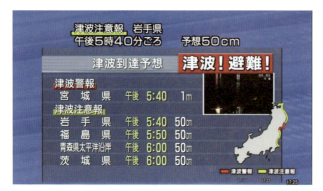

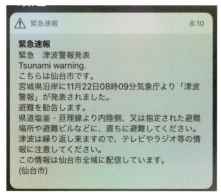

Evacuation drill

Tohoku University conducts a drill twice a year. A university-wide safety confirmation drill also takes place at the same time.

Tohoku University Safety Confirmation System

(1) Registering e-mail addresses
This system contacts all users by email, so you need only register your e-mail address to receive messages from the university. You can register via the Student Affairs Information System (students) or Integrated Electronic Authentication System (staff).
*Your address for the Digital Campus Mail (DC Mail, implemented October 2014) will already be registered in the Safety Confirmation System

Students: How to register via the Student Affairs Information System

Safety confirmation messages will be sent to the addresses you enter in "E-mail address 1" and "Forwarding address."

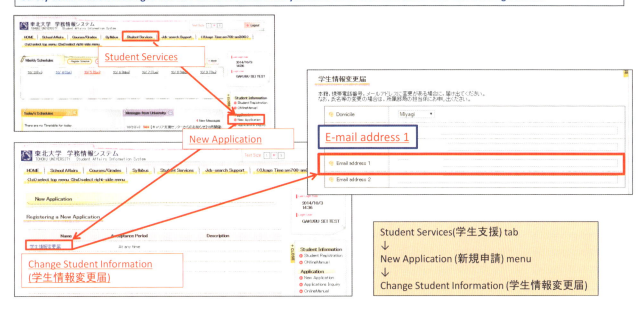

Student Services(学生支援) tab
↓
New Application (新規申請) menu
↓
Change Student Information (学生情報変更届)

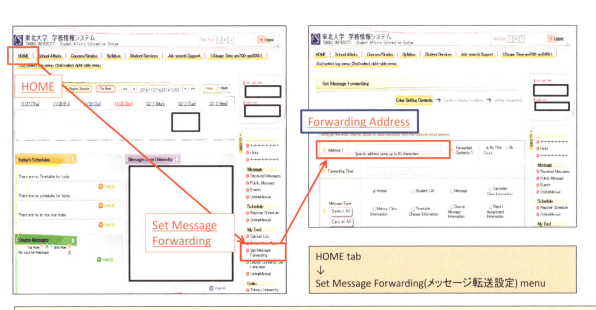

HOME tab
↓
Set Message Forwarding(メッセージ転送設定) menu

About forwarding addresses...
You can enter a forwarding address to receive information by e-mail, such as class cancellation notices.
Information from the Student Affairs Information System will be delivered according to your settings for content to be forwarded, delivery time, and message type.
In the case of emergencies or urgent notices, messages may be delivered at anytime, regardless of your delivery time setting.

* The mail address you enter will be registered in the Safety Confirmation System.
* If you are using a spam filter (particularly for your mobile phone) please whitelist the following addresses to ensure you can receive notifications.
  gkms-send@bureau.tohoku.ac.jp (sender's address for Student Affairs Information System)
  tohoku-univ@anpi.tohoku.ac.jp (sender's address for Safety Confirmation System)

(2) How to respond to e-mailed safety confirmation messages (example)

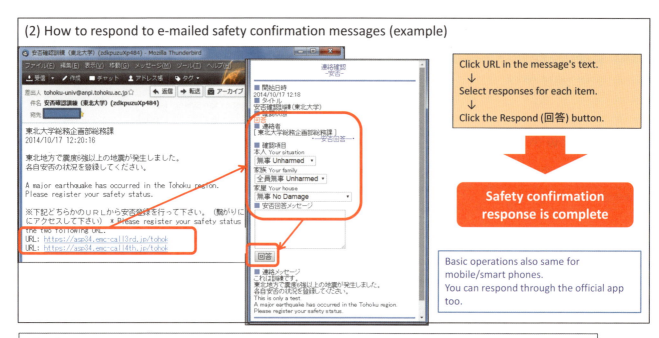

Click URL in the message's text.
↓
Select responses for each item.
↓
Click the Respond (回答) button.

Safety confirmation response is complete

Basic operations also same for mobile/smart phones.
You can respond through the official app too.

(3) Other

1. The sender's address will appear as tohoku-univ@anpi.tohoku.ac.jp
   Adjust your mail settings so you can receive messages from this domain.
2. If you receive no messages:
- Is your in-box full? → Free some space in your in-box.
- Is the message still on the mail server? → Run "Check for new messages" etc. on your mail client.
- Do you have a mail filter? → Add the domain to your filter's whitelist.

(4) How to register via the official app

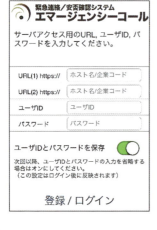

Download and install the free Emergency Call (エマージェンシーコール) app from the Apple App or Google Play Store. When configuring the connection settings, enter your Tohoku University ID and password to receive notifications from the app.
(If you change your Integrated Electronic Authentication System password, please change the password in the app as well.)

1. On the initial configuration screen, enter the below links, shown in blue, for URL (1) and URL (2).
   URL (1): https://asp34.emc-call3rd.jp/tohoku-univ
   URL (2): https://asp34.emc-call4th.jp/tohoku-univ

2. Enter your Tohoku University ID and password, then tap the "Register" button.
* We recommend turning on "Save user ID and password."

(3) The notification history screen will be displayed. This concludes initial setup.
(If you have no notification history, the screen will be blank.)

How to respond through the

*The format of notifications may differ depending on your device and settings.

Tap the received notification, or tap the app icon to start it, and enter your responses.

<Reference>Tohoku University (n.a.) Tohoku University Safety Confirmation System, http://www.bureau.tohoku.ac.jp/somu/saigaitaisaku/pdf/manual1-eng.pdf

6 Disaster Mitigation Action Card Game®
Earthquakes & Tsunamis

Objectives

- To be able to act properly when an earthquake happens.
- To think of many responses to earthquakes and tsunamis.

What is the Disaster Mitigation Action Card Game®?

DMAC is a game that teaches you how to protect yourself from disasters.

Roles

Game-Master: the organizer

Sub-Master: the facilitator

Player

How to Play

The Disaster Mitigation Action Card Game (DMAC) was created by students and their advisers in the Inter-Graduate School Doctoral Degree Program on Science for Global Safety. "Disaster Mitigation Action Card Game" is a registered trademark of Tohoku University.

7	Town Tour Challenge

Objectives

- To learn where to get daily necessities.
- To understand downtown Sendai better.

Welcome to Sendai! You might have already walked around the city, but now we would like to ask you to try this Town Tour Challenge to get to know the town better. Through this town tour, we hope you will enjoy walking around the downtown and become familiar with it. More importantly, we want Sendai to become your second hometown in the near future.

To pass this challenge, finish the following tasks:

*When you find a place through each task, please put a mark on the map.

1. Go to a store where you can buy food, medicine, and daily necessities, such as detergent and toilet paper, at one place. Take a group photo in front of the store.

   Store name:

2. You are planning a home party this weekend and want to get a lot of vegetables. Where can we get cheap and fresh vegetables? Go to the place and compare the prices with those in your country.

   Place:

   Vegetables in my country are [cheaper   /   more expensive   ] than there!

3. Do you have a mobile phone? Not yet? Please ask senior group members to show you where you can get one!

4. Go to the Sendai Tourist information desk and get information about tourist spots around Sendai.

5. Have you ever heard of a ¥100 shop (Hyakuen shop)? Go to a ¥100 shop, look around the shop, and find something interesting to you. Take a photo of it or buy it. Show it to other group members and decide who found the most interesting thing!

   Who found the most interesting thing in your group?:

6. You might need to buy some souvenirs when you go back to your country during holidays. Ask senior members what the most popular souvenir in Sendai is and where we can get them.

   What:

   Where:

7. Sometimes you might miss your country's food. Let's find a place where you can buy it!

   Store name:

   What can you buy there?:

8. You walked a lot! Do you feel tired? Let's have a cup of coffee. Please ask senior group members to take you to the best coffee shop in the town! Don't forget to take a selfie together!

   Coffee shop name:

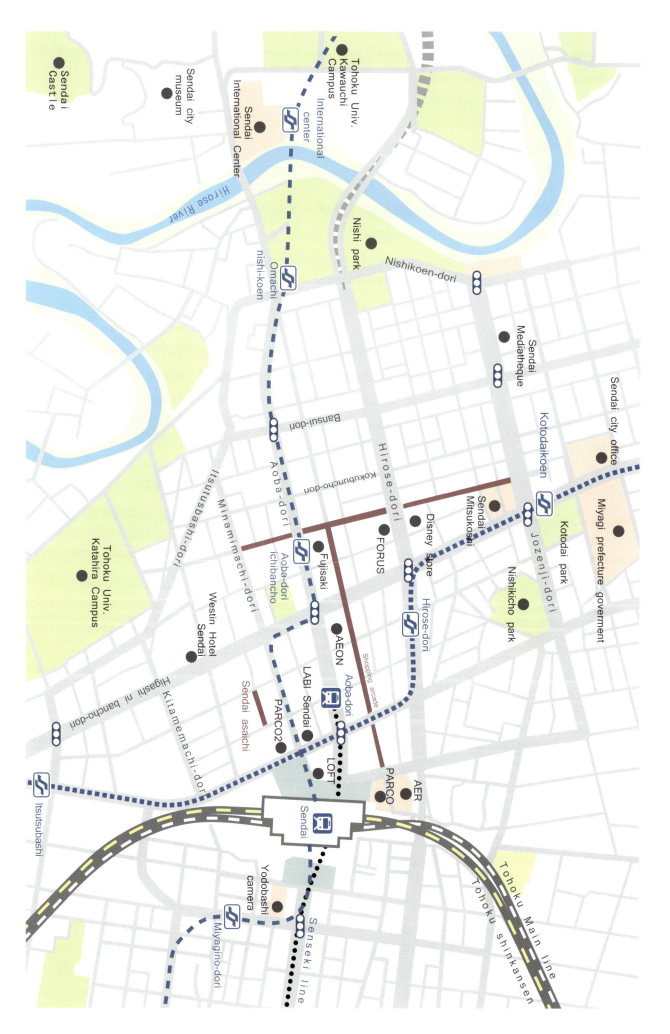

8 Useful Links

On campus

Global Learning Center
http://www.insc.tohoku.ac.jp/english/
Tohoku University Japanese Program
http://www.jlpk.ihe.tohoku.ac.jp
Center for Career Support
http://www.career.ihe.tohoku.ac.jp/english-home
Counseling Office, Center for Counseling and Disability Services
http://www.ccds.ihe.tohoku.ac.jp/front/counseling_office/sso_english/
Center for Learning Support
http://sla.cls.ihe.tohoku.ac.jp/english/
Tohoku University Library
http://www.library.tohoku.ac.jp/en/

Off campus

SenTIA (Sendai Tourism, Convention and International Association)
http://int.sentia-sendai.jp/e/
MIA (Miyagi International Association)
http://mia-miyagi.jp/english/index.html
SENDAI Tourist Information Desk
http://i-sendai.jp

How to ride and use a subway in Sendai

Sendai has two subways: the Namboku line and Tozai line. In the event of a disaster, please calmly evacuate the train or station as directed by the staff.

- Station entrances are indicated by the below symbol and signs showing the station name.
- These seats are priority seats for elderly persons, or those in need.
- Set your phone to silent mode and refrain from making telephone calls.
- Smoking is not allowed in stations and on trains.

Buy a ticket

Please purchase tickets at the ticket vending machines. The vending machines sell regular tickets, One-day Passes, icsca cards (new cards, excluding child and welfare discount cards), and icsca commuter passes (new adult commuter passes and renewed commuter passes —some exceptions apply). You can also add funds to your icsca card and print out your use history.

Board the subway

- All tickets on the subway are read via the automatic ticket gate. Please insert your ticket or pass into the slot, or touch your icsca card to the IC reader.

- On the Namboku Line, trains heading for Tomizawa stop at Platform 1, while trains heading for Izumi-chuo stop at Platform 2. On the Tozai Line, trains heading for Arai stop at Platform 1, while trains heading for Yagiyama Zoological Park stop at Platform 2. At the transfer hub in Sendai Station, trains heading for Arai stop at Platform 3, while trains heading for Yagiyama Zoological Park stop at Platform 4.

Caution ❶Please stand back from the platform gate. ❷Do not lean on the platform gate. ❸Do not lean over the platform gate or lean objects against the gate. ❹Please don't run to catch your train.

Get off the subway

- Please check the directions on the exit signs to find your way out. You can also use the elevators or escalators. Exit via the ticket gate.

- If you ride past your destination or your fare is insufficient, please ask at the station office next to the ticket gates.

References: Transportation Bureau, City of Sendai
http://www.kotsu.city.sendai.jp/english/subway/norikata.html

How to ride and use a public bus in Sendai

You board the bus from the middle and get off from the front.
Please pay the fare when you get of the bus.

You can ride both type of buses in the same way.

These seats are for aged people, pregnant women, and handicapped people.

Sendai city bus
Miyakoh bus

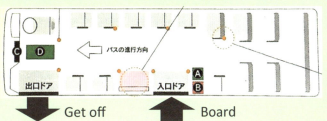
Get off | Board

If you cannot sit, please hold onto a handrail.

Board the bus

If using icsca
When boarding the bus, touch your icsca to the IC reader on the right side of the door.

If using one-day pass/cash
When boarding the bus, take a numbered ticket from the dispenser on the right side of the door.

Prepare fare/signal stop

● If using a one-day pass or cash, check the number on your numbered ticket and prepare the fare amount that is shown for that number on the display at the front of the bus.

●When the bus leaves the stop before your destination, push the signal button.

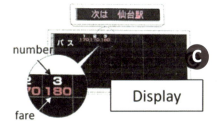
In this case, if your ticket number is 3, you will pay 180 yen.

Get off the bus

If using icsca
When getting off the bus, touch your icsca card to the IC reader near the driver's seat to pay.
If the remaining balance on the icsca card is too little, you can add funds to your card on the bus.

If using one-day pass/cash
Insert the numbered ticket into the fare box. The fare is shown on the screen. No change can be given, so please use the change machine at the front of the bus before paying if necessary.

If you lose something on the bus, call the **Sendai lost and found office 022-223-4812**

References: Transportation Bureau, City of Sendai
https://www.kotsu.city.sendai.jp/english/bus/norikata.html

Discount Passes and Tickets

Gakuto Sendai City Bus/Subway Free Pass

All students are eligible for the "Gakuto Sendai City Bus/Subway Free Pass". These passes are for students who go to university by bus, subway, or by bus and subway. The passes are available for non-regular students too. Pass types are as follows.

Adult (junior high school and older)	Type	1-month	3-month	6-month
City Bus Free Pass	City Bus Only	JPY5,140	JPY15,420	JPY30,840
Subway Free Pass	Nanboku Line	JPY6,950	JPY20,850	JPY41,700
	Tozai Line	JPY6,950	JPY20,850	JPY41,700
	Nanboku Line and Tozai Line	JPY8,340	JPY25,020	JPY50,040
City Bus and Subway Free Pass	City Bus and Nanboku Line	JPY10,280	JPY30,840	JPY61,680
	City Bus and Tozai Line	JPY10,280	JPY30,840	JPY61,680
	City Bus, Nanboku Line, and Tozai Line	JPY11,460	JPY34,380	JPY68,760

How to purchase a pass (first time)

❶ Request a Student Commuter Certificate (Tsugaku Shomeisho) at the university
・For 3rd-year undergraduates and above:
➡ contact the Registrar at your faculty.
・For 1st- and 2nd-year undergraduate students:
➡ go to service window No.4, Education and Student Support Center, Kawauchi-Kita Campus.
・Non-regular students (ex. research, special research, special auditing students):
➡ contact the Registrar at your faculty.
❷ Visit a designated ticket office and submit the Certificate and a completed icsca school commuter pass application form "icsca Tsugaku Teikiken Konyu Moshikomisho". (You can purchase the pass up to 7 days prior to your desired date of use).

IC card "icsca"
With an icsca card, you can use the bus and subway systems smoothly.

How to renew an existing pass

❶ Visit a designated ticket office and show them your existing pass and Student ID card. (You can renew the pass up to 14 days prior to the expiration date of your old pass.)
You must present a Student Commuter Certificate (Tsugaku Shomeisho) once per school year after the first purchase.

The icsca school commuter pass application form (icsca Tsugaku Teikiken Konyu Moshikomisho) is available at designated ticket offices. You can also download it from the Sendai City Transportation Bureau Website. If you download and fill out the form in advance, your application will go more smoothly.

Designated ticket offices:
You can find ticket offices at: Izumi-chuo Station, Kotodai-koen Station, Sendai Station, Nagamachi-minami Station, Yagiyama-dobutsu-koen Station, Yakushido Station, Arai Station, Asahigaoka Bus Terminal, and the Transportation Bureau.
Bus offices are located at: Kasuminome, Sanezawa, Higashi-Sendai and Shirasawa.

MEMO

MEMO